THIS B...
BELON...

C000111901

Name: Age.

Favourite player:

2020/21

My Predictions...   **Actual...**

The Seagulls' final position:

The Seagulls' top scorer:

Premier League winners:

Premier League top scorer:

FA Cup winners:

EFL Cup winners:

Contributors: Peter Rogers, Luke Nicoli.

A TWOCAN PUBLICATION

©2020. Published by twocan under licence from Brighton & Hove Albion FC.

ISBN 978-1-913362-27-0

PICTURE CREDITS: Brighton and Hove Albion FC, Paul Hazlewood, Action Images and Press Association.

£9

3

CONTENTS

MATY 01
RYAN

POSITION: Goalkeeper   **DOB:** 08.04.92
NATIONALITY: Australian

Albion's first-choice keeper for the past three seasons in the Premier League, he has now made over 100 appearances for the Seagulls.

Since his arrival from Spanish club Valencia in 2017 he has pulled off a number of key saves, with his favourite being a late penalty save against Stoke City's Charlie Adam in February 2018, which earned Albion a crucial point.

TARIQ 02
LAMPTEY

POSITION: Defender   **DOB:** 30.09.00
NATIONALITY : English

The England U21 international joined the Albion in January 2020 from Chelsea, where he made his professional debut the previous month, in the Blues' 2-1 win at Arsenal.

He had to wait until June to make his Seagulls debut, at Leicester City, but caught the eye with a barnstorming performance at right-back and has continued to impress for Graham Potter's side.

03 BEN
WHITE

POSITION: Defender   **DOB:** 08.10.97
NATIONALITY : English

The former Albion academy player made his professional debut on loan at Newport County, against Southend United, in August 2017.

He has since had loan spells at Peterborough United and Leeds United, helping the Elland Road club to the Championship title last season.

Returning to the Amex, he made his Premier League bow on the opening day of this season against Chelsea.

LEWIS

DUNK

SOCCER SKILLS

Great goalkeepers are an essential ingredient for successful teams in today's game. They have to excel in all areas of the art of 'keeping and Mat Ryan is a great 'keeper who lives up to these expectations.

DISTRIBUTION
THE BASICS OF A GOOD THROWING TECHNIQUE

OVERARM THROW

This is best for covering long distances. The body should be in line with the direction of the throw, with the weight on the back foot. The ball should be brought forward in a bowling action with the arm straight.

JAVELIN THROW

This throw is made quickly with a low trajectory. The arm is bent for this throw, the ball is held beside the head, and the body is in line with the direction of the throw. The arm is brought forward in a pushing movement with the ball being released at the top.

UNDERARM THROW

The ball is released from a crouching position, with a smooth underarm swing.

Throws do not usually travel as far as kicks but the greater speed and accuracy of throwing can make up for the lack of distance and will help the team retain possession. A player receiving a throw must be able to control it early.

Work hard at distribution and the benefits of this will be seen whenever you are in possession during a match.

EXERCISE ONE

Grab a friend and throw the ball to each other using the various throwing techniques at various distances apart.

EXERCISE TWO

The goalkeeper with the ball uses the various throws to knock another ball off a marker.

EXERCISE THREE

The goalkeepers try to throw the ball through the markers using various throwing techniques.

BOYS OF '11

With the new Amex Stadium set to open in the summer of 2011, Albion's former home at Withdean couldn't have wished for a better send off with the League One title-winning campaign of 2010/11.

In Gus Poyet's first full season as boss, the Seagulls were far from favourites to win the title, with the likes of former top-flight clubs Southampton, Sheffield Wednesday and Charlton Athletic tipped to mount a promotion push.

Albion, however, had ended the previous season strongly and an opening-day win at Swindon Town set the tone for the campaign ahead.

With the likes of future Premier League players Glenn Murray, Elliott Bennett, Ashley Barnes, Liam Bridcutt and Chris Wood in the side, Albion were a model of consistency, losing just twice at the 'Theatre of Trees' all season.

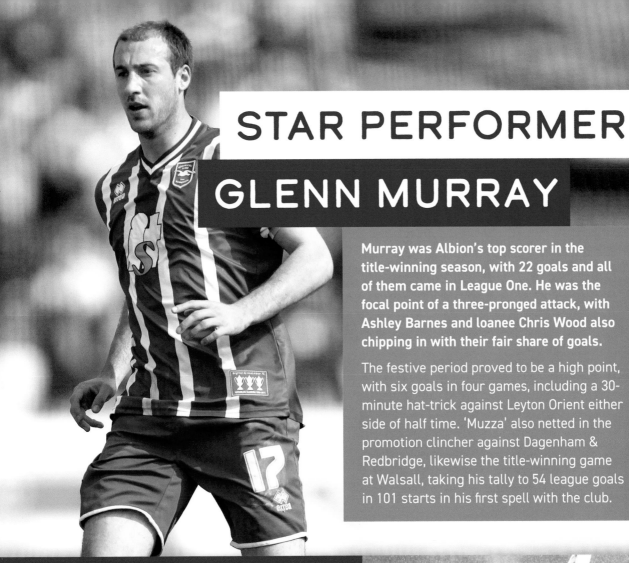

STAR PERFORMER
GLENN MURRAY

Murray was Albion's top scorer in the title-winning season, with 22 goals and all of them came in League One. He was the focal point of a three-pronged attack, with Ashley Barnes and loanee Chris Wood also chipping in with their fair share of goals.

The festive period proved to be a high point, with six goals in four games, including a 30-minute hat-trick against Leyton Orient either side of half time. 'Muzza' also netted in the promotion clincher against Dagenham & Redbridge, likewise the title-winning game at Walsall, taking his tally to 54 league goals in 101 starts in his first spell with the club.

There were a number of highlights along the way, with a 4-0 win at Charlton in October laying down a real marker that the side were in it for the long haul, while a Tuesday night draw at Southampton the following month also showed the side's mettle.

Yet it was a 12-game unbeaten run in the second half of the season, including eight straight victories, which took the team to the verge of promotion. It came on a memorable mid-April night at Withdean, against relegation-threatened Dagenham and Redbridge, with the Seagulls securing an edgy 4-3 victory.

Promotion had been secured with five games to spare, while the title was clinched four days later with a 3-1 win at Walsall.

Bring on the Championship and bring on the Amex!

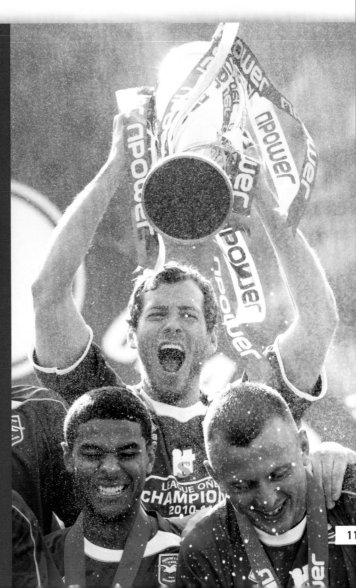

ADAM `04` WEBSTER

POSITION: Defender   **DOB:** 04.01.95
NATIONALITY : English

The former Portsmouth trainee made over 80 appearances for the club before joining Ipswich Town in 2016.

Two years later he moved to fellow Championship side Bristol City, where he was named Player of the Year in his one season with the Robins. His form secured a move to the Albion in August 2019 and he has since emerged as a mainstay of Graham Potter's defence.

LEWIS `05` DUNK

POSITION: Defender   **DOB:** 21.11.91
NATIONALITY: English

Brighton born and bred, the centre-back took over the captain's armband from Bruno at the start of the 2019/20 season.

A model of consistency, he continues to lead by example and has shown the form that won him an England cap, against the United States, in 2018. He made his 300th club appearance against Manchester United in June - ten years after his Albion debut.

AARON 07
CONNOLLY

POSITION: Striker   **DOB:** 28.01.00
NATIONALITY: Irish

The academy graduate netted his first goal for the club in the EFL Cup at Bristol Rovers in August 2019, but really made headlines two months later when he netted twice in a 3-0 win against Tottenham at the Amex.

He was a rewarded with a debut for the Republic of Ireland against Georgia the following week, and has maintained a place in the senior squad for both club and country.

YVES 08
BISSOUMA

POSITION: Midfielder   **DOB:** 30.08.96
NATIONALITY: Malian

With nearly 50 Ligue 1 appearances to his name at Lille, the central midfielder moved to the Albion in July 2018.

He found it difficult to command a regular place initially - but emerged as a regular in the second half of the 2019/20 season. He has also endeared himself to Albion fans with a couple of spectacular goals this past year, at Burnley and Everton.

13

GOAL OF THE SEASON

ALIREZA JAHANBAKHSH

V CHELSEA

1 JANUARY 2020

Arguably the most spectacular goal ever seen at the Amex, AJ's bicycle kick on New Year's Day against Chelsea was the perfect way to see in 2020.

With just six minutes left in the game and the Albion trailing 1-0, a Leandro Trossard corner was headed back into the heart of the box by Lewis Dunk. Jahanbakhsh instinctively swivelled on the spot to send his overhead kick beyond a sea of bodies while leaving Blues 'keeper Kepa Arrizabalaga rooted to the spot.

It was the Iranian midfielder's second goal in as many games, having netted in the 2-0 home win against Bournemouth, and he collapsed in sheer emotion before being brought to his feet again by ecstatic team-mates.

"That was the best goal I've scored in my career," he recalls. "When I saw the ball, I just tried to hit it as hard as I could and the bicycle kick was the only option.

"I've done this before in training but to do it in an important competition against such a big team was amazing. When Lewis Dunk headed the ball back, I just set myself to hit it as hard as I could.

"It couldn't have gone any better and you could see by the look on my face that I could not believe it!

"It had been a disappointing season for me to that point, but to score that goal and in quick succession to the other shows you just how quickly things can turn around in football. I was delighted to help the team to four important points."

RUNNERS-UP

YVES BISSOUMA V BURNLEY

A late runner for the main award, Biss scored his spectacular effort on the final day of last season at Burnley.

Having won the ball with a sliding tackle as the hosts broke forward, the ball cannoned back into his path off the Clarets' rearguard and he let fly with a superb 25-yard effort that flew into the top corner of Nick Pope's net.

YVES BISSOUMA V EVERTON

Yves clearly likes his trips to the north west as he netted another long-range effort against Everton in October.

With the game all but over, the midfielder scored a fine consolation goal when he picked up a cushioned header from Solly March some 25 yards out. In one movement he controlled the ball on his chest, swivelled and let fly with a right-foot volley that left Jordan Pickford clutching at thin air.

ADULTS

Who is the captain of Wolverhampton Wanderers?

1 ANSWER

Can you name the four Premier League clubs that reached the 2019/20 FA Cup semi-finals?

2 ANSWER

At which club did Chelsea boss Frank Lampard begin his managerial career?

3 ANSWER

Who is the oldest manager in the Premier League?

4 ANSWER

At which club did Southampton's star striker Danny Ings begin his career?

5 ANSWER

From which club did Manchester United sign Bruno Fernandes?

6 ANSWER

At which club did Newcastle manager Steve Bruce begin his playing career?

7 ANSWER

How many clubs from the north west have won the Premier League title?

8 ANSWER

Who were the first London club to win the Premier League?

9 ANSWER

Which Premier League manager is also his club's record goalscorer?

10 ANSWER

V KIDS

Challenge your favourite grown-up and find out which of you is the biggest Premier League brain! The adults' questions are on the left page and the kids' questions are on the right page.

Which team began the 2020/21 season as Premier League champions for the first time?

1 ANSWER

What nationality is Chelsea striker Timo Werner?

2 ANSWER

How many Premier League clubs have the title 'United' in their name?

3 ANSWER

Who plays their home games at Molineux?

4 ANSWER

Which Premier League ground has the largest capacity?

5 ANSWER

Which current Premier League club won last season's League Cup?

6 ANSWER

What is Everton's nickname?

7 ANSWER

Can you name the club that play their home matches at St James' Park?

8 ANSWER

Who is the manager of Leicester City?

9 ANSWER

What nationality is Tottenham Hotspur manager Jose Mourinho?

10 ANSWER

Fill the page with your footy goals and dreams, no matter how big or small, and then start working on how to accomplish them!

We've started you off...

1. Visit the American Express Community Stadium

2. Complete 50 keepy-uppies

FOOTY BUCKET LIST

YVES
BISSOUMA

ANSWERS ON PAGE 62

WHO ARE YA?

Can you figure out the identity of all these Seagulls stars?

5

6

7

8

9

10

11

21

NEAL **09**
MAUPAY

POSITION: Striker   **DOB:** 14.08.96
NATIONALITY: French

The former France U21 international caught the eye at Brentford, where he scored 41 goals in 95 games.

Having netted 25 Championship goals in 2018/19, he moved to the Seagulls and capped his debut with a goal in the 3-0 win at Watford on the opening day. He also netted a memorable winner against Arsenal on the return to action following Project Restart, and scored four goals in five games at the start of this season.

ALEXIS **10**
MAC ALLISTER

POSITION: Midfielder   **DOB:** 24.12.98
NATIONALITY: Argentinean

Arriving from Argentinos Juniors in January 2019, the midfield playmaker was immediately loaned back to his former club, then spent the first half of 2019/20 at Boca Juniors.

Impressing at the Argentine giants, he also made his international debut before a return to the Seagulls, where he made his bow in the 0-0 draw against Wolves in March 2020.

LEANDRO TROSSARD **11**

POSITION: Midfielder **DOB:** 04.12.94
NATIONALITY: Belgian

Named as the Belgian league's Player of the Year, having scored 22 goals with Genk in 2018/19, the winger moved to the Amex last summer.

He enjoyed a dream debut, scoring in a 1-1 draw with West Ham, and also had a goal disallowed by VAR. He went from strength to strength in 2020, scoring fine goals against Norwich and Liverpool following Project Restart.

PREPARING
FOR ACTION

Football matches may well be scheduled for 90 minutes but there are many days of preparation that go into making sure that Graham Potter's men are at their physical and mental peak when they cross the white line to represent Brighton & Hove Albion.

Like all Premier League clubs, the Seagulls' pre-match planning is meticulous. The manager of course has the final say as to who makes his starting line-up but the boss is ably assisted by a backroom staff of coaches, sports scientists, strength and conditioning experts, physiotherapists and nutritionists, who all play their part in helping fine tune the players ahead of the manager's team selection.

The majority of the squad's preparations take place at the club's training ground and that all begins when the players report back for pre-season training.

Although the modern-day player has little down-time in terms of maintaining his overall fitness, pre-season really is a vital time for footballers to build themselves up to remain as fit, strong and healthy as possible for the challenging season that awaits.

The pre-season schedule often begins with a series of fitness tests. The results of those tests enables the club's coaching and fitness staff to assess each player's condition and level of fitness, to ensure they are given the right workload during the pre-season programme.

When it comes to winning football matches, it is well known that both hard work and practice are two essential ingredients to success. However, in terms of strength and fitness, then rest, recovery and diet also have crucial parts to play in a footballer's wellbeing.

The modern game now sees technology playing its part in training too. Prior to beginning their training sessions, the players are provided with a GPS tracking system and heart-rate analysis monitors, ensuring that all that they do in a training session can be measured, monitored and reviewed.

On-pitch training drills and gym work are now enhanced further with players often taking part in yoga and pilates classes while always receiving expert advice in terms of their diet, rest and mental welfare.

ALEXIS
MAC ALLISTER

SOCCER SKILLS
DEFENDING

Defending is an art - not as spectacular as swerving a free kick around the wall into the net or floating a crossfield pass into the path of an oncoming wing-back - but nevertheless, just as important. Every successful team has a solid defence and can defend as a unit.

Defenders must also master the art of defending one on one...

EXERCISE ONE

Two adjacent 10m x 10m grids have two players, X and Y at the opposite ends of the grids. X plays the ball to Y, who is then allowed to attack defender X with the ball. Y's target is to be able to stop the ball, under control, on the opposite end line. Defender X has to try to stop this happening. Y is encouraged to be direct and run at X with the ball.

KEY FACTORS

1. Do not approach the attacker square on. Adopt a sideways stance which enables rapid forward and backwards movement.
2. Do not dive in. Be patient and wait for your opponent to make a mistake. Always be on your toes.
3. Threaten the ball without actually committing to a tackle. Pretending to tackle can often panic the opponent!
4. Tackle when you are sure you will win it!

EXERCISE TWO

Here the game is progressed to a two v two situation when X1 and X2 play as a team against Y1 and Y2.

The same target is used for this game - the players have to stand on the opposite line with the ball, either by dribbling past their opponents or by passing the ball through them.

The same key factors are relevant here with the addition of two more:

5. Covering your defending partner when he is being attacked.
6. Communication between the two defenders is vital.

If a team can get these points of defending right, throughout the side, they will become very difficult to beat.

Take our quick-fire personality test to see where Graham Potter would utilise your skills in the Seagulls' line-up...

WHICH FOOTBALLER

ARE YOU?

1. What is your favourite activity at the park?

a. Leaping around

b. Practicing my heading

c. Lots of non-stop running

d. Scoring goals

2. What is your biggest strength?

a. My height

b. My strength

c. My stamina

d. My speed

3. Which would you rather win?

a. A game of catch

b. A weight lifting contest

c. A long distance run

d. A sprint race

4. You score a goal! How do you celebrate?

a. I turn and punch the air

b. I clench my fist in delight

c. I high-five a teammate

d. I slide on my knees

5. How would the opposition describe you?

a. Hard to beat

b. Determined to succeed

c. All-action

d. Lethal in front of goal

6. What's your favourite move?

a. Springing high to catch under pressure

b. A sliding tackle

c. Playing the perfect through ball

d. Spinning away from my marker

7. What is the key to winning a game?

a. Keeping a clean sheet

b. Winning your individual battles

c. Maintaining possession

d. Taking chances that come your way

8. What is your favourite number?

a. One

b. Five

c. Seven

d. Nine

9. How would you describe your style of play?

a. Disciplined

b. Fully committed

c. Relentless

d. Technically gifted

10. What do your teammates call you?

a. Secure

b. Reliable

c. Energetic

d. Mr/Miss goals

MOSTLY As

You would clearly be a safe pair of hands in goal. Watch out Mat Ryan, there's competition here for the No1 shirt!

MOSTLY Bs

Sounds like you are a young Adam Webster in the making - there could well be a role for you in the Seagulls' back four...

MOSTLY Cs

You could comfortably take your place in the heart of midfield and help make things tick at the Amex. Move over Alexis Mac Allister!

MOSTLY Ds

Looks like we have a budding Neal Maupay on our hands! Who do you fancy partnering in attack?

TEAM 20/21

ADAM 14
LALLANA

POSITION: Midfielder   **DOB:** 10.05.88
NATIONALITY : English

The experienced England international became Albion's first signing of the summer, having arrived from Premier League champions Liverpool.

During his time at Anfield he also won Champions League, Super Cup and World Club Cup honours and in 2016 he was named England Player of the Year. He has returned to the south coast having started his career at Southampton, where he made over 260 appearances.

PASCAL 13
GROSS

POSITION: Midfielder   **DOB:** 15.06.91
NATIONALITY: German

A versatile midfielder who can play behind the lead striker or out wide, Pascal has now racked up over a century of Albion appearances.

Arriving from Ingolstadt ahead of the club's Premier League debut in 2017, he has scored a number of important goals - including Albion's second in the epic 3-3 draw at West Ham in February 2020.

ALIREZA 16 JAHANBAKHSH

POSITION: Midfielder **DOB:** 11.08.93
NATIONALITY: Iranian

With 34 goals in 79 league starts for Dutch side AZ Alkmaar, Alireza joined the Seagulls in July 2018 and made 24 appearances in his debut season.

The Iran international found chances limited in 2019/20 but showed flashes of his undoubted ability, scoring against Bournemouth in late December then following up with his superb bicycle-kick goal against Chelsea on New Year's Day.

He also netted two fine goals, against Portsmouth and Preston, in this season's Carabao Cup.

STEVEN 17 ALZATE

POSITION: Midfielder **DOB:** 08.09.98
NATIONALITY: Colombian

Like Aaron Connolly, the midfielder enjoyed a successful breakthrough 2019/20 season with the Seagulls. A former Leyton Orient youngster, he made his Premier League debut at Newcastle United in September 2019, earning the Man of the Match award.

Playing on the right side of midfield or as a wing-back, he made over 20 appearances in 2019/20 and became a full Colombia international.

While Albion's second season in the FA Women's Super League was curtailed due to the coronavirus pandemic, Hope Powell's side made plenty of progress.

The Seagulls had finished the previous campaign in ninth place with 16 points after 20 games, and while the 2019/20 campaign saw the side sitting in the same position, they had amassed 13 points with four games still to play.

Powell had moved to strengthen her side by bringing in the Netherlands international defender Danique Kerkdijk, likewise French midfielder Lea Le Garrec, and both emerged as key players over the course of the campaign.

Also pleasing for Powell would have been the form of forward Kayleigh Green, who had netted six goals in all competitions, likewise Aileen Whelan, who had netted five times in FA WSL games.

The opening weeks proved difficult but with the side handed the opportunity to play at the Amex for the visit of Birmingham in mid-November, rather than their usual home at Crawley Town, the side responded with an excellent 3-0 win - the highlight being a stunning long-range effort from the now-departed Le Garrec.

The win came on the back of a shock Continental Cup win against WSL holders Arsenal on penalties and both wins certainly provided the side with a confidence boost heading into the festive period, where Liverpool were beaten 1-0.

Merseyside rivals Everton were defeated by the same scoreline in February, while Powell's side performed admirably to hold high-flying newcomers Manchester United to a 1-1 draw.

Albion had also made progress to the quarter-finals of the FA Cup before the season was curtailed, leaving Powell enthused for the current season, with the arrival of Dutch international Inessa Kaagman, fellow midfielder Nora Heroum from AC Milan, South Korea World Cup star Lee Geum-min, Republic of Ireland international Denise O'Sullivan and New Zealand player of the year Rebekah Stott.

"Since the start of 2020 especially, I felt we had improved considerably," she reflected. "We carried more of an attacking threat, got some important wins against Liverpool and Everton, and deservedly held Manchester United, who have one of the stronger squads in the WSL.

"We started this season well with a win against Birmingham and a notable 0-0 draw at Manchester City, so there's plenty to look forward to with this group of players."

WOMEN'S TEAM

COLOUR

LEANDRO
TROSSARD

ADAM
LALLANA

PLAYER
OF THE SEASON

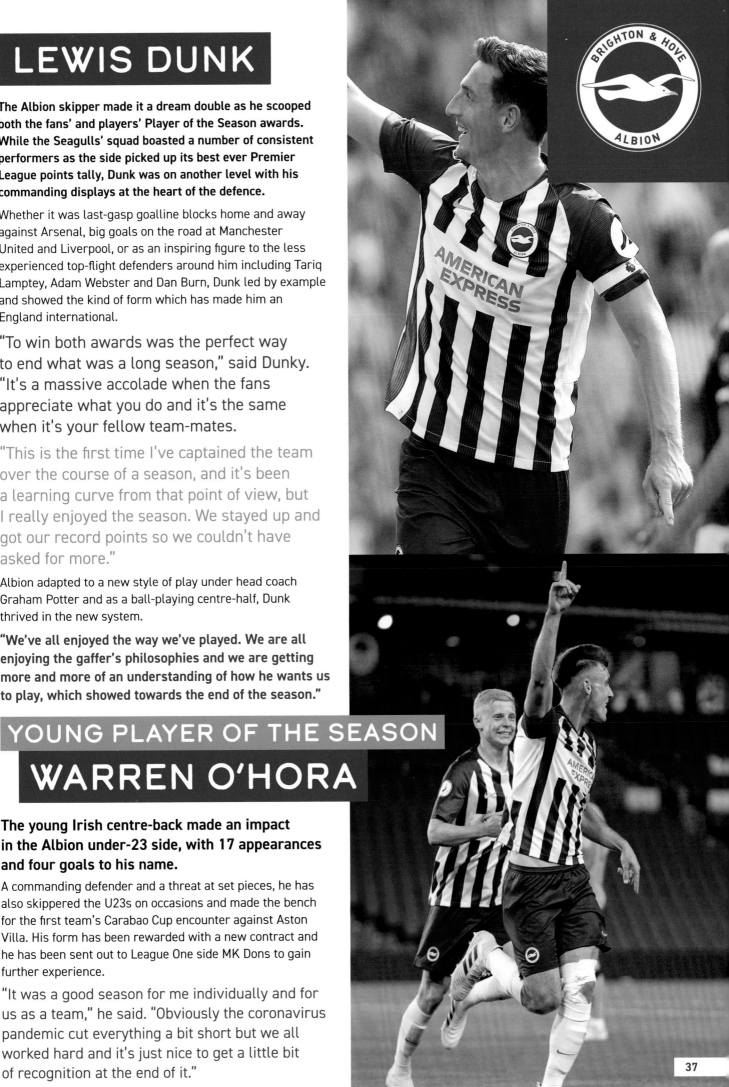

LEWIS DUNK

The Albion skipper made it a dream double as he scooped both the fans' and players' Player of the Season awards. While the Seagulls' squad boasted a number of consistent performers as the side picked up its best ever Premier League points tally, Dunk was on another level with his commanding displays at the heart of the defence.

Whether it was last-gasp goalline blocks home and away against Arsenal, big goals on the road at Manchester United and Liverpool, or as an inspiring figure to the less experienced top-flight defenders around him including Tariq Lamptey, Adam Webster and Dan Burn, Dunk led by example and showed the kind of form which has made him an England international.

"To win both awards was the perfect way to end what was a long season," said Dunky. "It's a massive accolade when the fans appreciate what you do and it's the same when it's your fellow team-mates.

"This is the first time I've captained the team over the course of a season, and it's been a learning curve from that point of view, but I really enjoyed the season. We stayed up and got our record points so we couldn't have asked for more."

Albion adapted to a new style of play under head coach Graham Potter and as a ball-playing centre-half, Dunk thrived in the new system.

"We've all enjoyed the way we've played. We are all enjoying the gaffer's philosophies and we are getting more and more of an understanding of how he wants us to play, which showed towards the end of the season."

YOUNG PLAYER OF THE SEASON
WARREN O'HORA

The young Irish centre-back made an impact in the Albion under-23 side, with 17 appearances and four goals to his name.

A commanding defender and a threat at set pieces, he has also skippered the U23s on occasions and made the bench for the first team's Carabao Cup encounter against Aston Villa. His form has been rewarded with a new contract and he has been sent out to League One side MK Dons to gain further experience.

"It was a good season for me individually and for us as a team," he said. "Obviously the coronavirus pandemic cut everything a bit short but we all worked hard and it's just nice to get a little bit of recognition at the end of it."

JOSE 19
IZQUIERDO

POSITION: Striker **DOB:** 07.07.92
NATIONALITY: Colombian

The winger arrived from Club Brugge in August 2017 and quickly became a fans' favourite with his marauding runs and eye-catching goals - most notably against West Ham and Stoke City.

A knee injury caused the Colombia international to miss the entire 2019/20 season but he returned to action in October - some 17 months after he last kicked a ball in anger for the Seagulls.

SOLLY 20
MARCH

POSITION: Midfielder **DOB:** 20.07.94
NATIONALITY: English

With one appearance for non-league Lewes to his name, Solly joined the Albion in 2011 and made his debut against Derby County in August 2013.

The left winger now has over 180 appearances to his name - a high point being the promotion clincher against Wigan in 2017, where he scored. The former England U21 international suffered with injury issues in 2019/20 but has been a regular fixture this season..

21 FLORIN ANDONE

POSITION: Striker **DOB:** 11.04.93
NATIONALITY: Romanian

The striker arrived from Spanish side Deportivo La Coruna in 2018 and netted on his first start for the Seagulls, against Huddersfield Town.

He then scored in the next game, a fine individual goal against Crystal Palace, before joining Galatasaray on loan for the 2019/20 season.

The Romanian international has since been sidelined by two knee injuries.

JASON 23 STEELE

POSITION: Goalkeeper **DOB:** 18.08.90
NATIONALITY: English

The experienced former Middlesbrough and Blackburn Rovers keeper joined the Seagulls in 2018 after a spell at Sunderland.

He made his debut in the FA Cup against Bournemouth in January 2019, and followed up with further impressive performances against Portsmouth and Preston in this season's Carabao Cup.

CLASSIC
FANTASTIC

ANSWERS ON PAGE 62

Gully, the Albion mascot, is hiding in five places as Seagulls fans celebrate winning the Division Two Play-Off final at the Millennium Stadium in 2004. Can you find him?

BRIGHTON & HOVE ALBION

BEN WHITE

Can you find the eight differences between these two photos?

SPOT THE DIFFERENCE

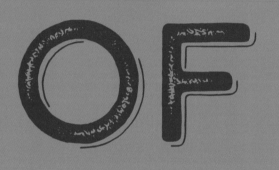

BOYS OF '83

The Seagulls' class of 1983 wrote their names into Brighton & Hove Albion folklore as they took the club to Wembley for the first time ever with Jimmy Melia's men reaching the holy grail of the FA Cup final.

Brighton's trip to the Twin Towers began with a third-round tie at home to Newcastle United. After the match ended 1-1, the Seagulls progressed to the fourth round following a 1-0 win at St James' Park with Peter Ward on target in the replay.

The fourth-round meeting with First Division rivals Manchester City gave Melia's men their most comprehensive win of the run as they brushed City aside 4-0 at the Goldstone Ground.

Against all odds, the Seagulls pulled off a memorable fifth-round victory over league champions Liverpool at Anfield before Norwich City were beaten 1-0 in the quarter-final at the Goldstone.

STAR PERFORMER
JIMMY CASE

Case's goals proved to be a major factor in the Seagulls reaching the 1983 FA Cup final.

The fans' favourite struck on four occasions on the road to Wembley. He first netted in the 4-0 fourth-round rout of Manchester City at the Goldstone. The ex-Liverpool man then stunned his former employers by scoring the winning goal in Albion's shock 2-1 win at Anfield. His third goal of the campaign proved to be the difference between Brighton and Norwich City at the quarter-final stage, and the experienced midfield man then opened the scoring in the semi-final success over Sheffield Wednesday, with a stunning long-range effort at Highbury.

With Wembley almost in touching distance, Brighton was gripped by cup fever and just Second Division Sheffield Wednesday stood between Albion and a first Wembley appearance.

Goals from Jimmy Case and Michael Robinson booked the Seagulls their place in the end-of-season showpiece with a 2-1 semi-final victory over the Owls at Highbury.

In front of 100,000 at Wembley and the watching nation, Manchester United provided the cup final opposition on a truly unforgettable day in the Seagulls' history.

Gordon Smith put Brighton in front before United struck back to lead 2-1. A dramatic 85th-minute equaliser from Gary Stevens to the match to extra-time but the two sides could not be separated. Sadly the replay proved to be a bridge too far as United ran out comfortable winners.

45

DAVY 24 PROPPER

POSITION: Midfielder   **DOB:** 02.09.91
NATIONALITY: Dutch

The Netherlands international has been a regular at the heart of the Seagulls' midfield since arriving from PSV Eindhoven in August 2017.

Indeed, he has made over 100 appearances, forming a solid partnership with the departed Dale Stephens for many of those games. He has also maintained his place in the Dutch squad throughout his time at the Amex.

26 ROBERT SANCHEZ

POSITION: Goalkeeper   **DOB:** 18.11.97
NATIONALITY: Spanish

Joining the club's academy at the age of 15, he made his professional debut on loan at Forest Green Rovers, against Grimsby, in August 2018.

Robert spent last season on loan at League One Rochdale and put in a particularly eye-catching performance against Manchester United in the Carabao Cup.

29 ANDI ZEQIRI

POSITION: Striker **DOB:** 22.06.91
NATIONALITY: Kosovan

Andi joined his local club Lausanne in 2015 and went on to score 35 goals in 104 appearances before his move to the Seagulls.

A former Switzerland U21 international, he scored nine goals in nine games at that level but having obtained a Kosovan passport, he has stated his intention to play for the country of his parents' birthplace.

30 BERNARDO

POSITION: Defender **DOB:** 14.05.95
NATIONALITY: Brazilian

Signed as a utility defender from RB Leipzig in July 2018, Bernardo has featured mainly as a left-back during his time at the Amex.

While he has found opportunities more limited than he would have liked, the Brazilian still made 26 Premier League appearances in his first two seasons.

He is the son of former Bayern Munich and Brazil international Bernardo Fernandes da Silva.

31 CHRISTIAN WALTON

POSITION: Goalkeeper **DOB:** 09.11.95
NATIONALITY: English

Joining Albion's academy from his hometown club Plymouth in 2013, Christian made his Albion debut in a League Cup tie at Tottenham the following year, aged just 18.

He has since enjoyed extended loan spells at Luton Town, Wigan Athletic and Blackburn Rovers - helping the Latics to the League One title in 2017/18.

He is a former England U21 international.

NEAL

MAUPAY

SOCCER SKILLS
CHEST CONTROL

Controlling the ball quickly and with minimum fuss in order to get the ball where you want it, so you can pass or shoot, can be the difference between a good player and a top class player.

EXERCISE ONE

Grab two of your mates to start the exercise. A and C stand 10 yards apart and have a ball each, ready to act as servers.

B works first. B must run towards A who serves the ball for B to control with the chest and pass back to A. B then turns, runs to C and repeats the exercise.

Once B has worked for 30 seconds all the players rotate.

KEY FACTORS

1. Look to control the ball as early as possible.

2. Get in line with the ball.

3. Keep eyes on the ball.

4. Relax the body on impact with the ball to cushion it.

EXERCISE TWO

In this exercise there are 5 servers positioned around a 15-yard square. At one side of the square there is a goal.

T starts in the middle of the square. S1 serves first, throwing the ball in the air towards T. T must control the ball with the chest and try to shoot past the goalkeeper. As soon as T has shot on goal they must prepare for the next serve from S2.

Once T has received a ball from every server the players rotate positions - the same key factors apply.

Players who can control a ball quickly, putting the ball in a position for a shot or pass, give themselves and their teammates the extra valuable seconds required in today's intense style of play.

49

ADULTS

Which other Premier League club has Everton boss Carlo Ancelotti previously been in charge of?

11 ANSWER

Who is the current longest-serving manager in the Premier League?

12 ANSWER

From which then non-league club did Leicester City sign Jamie Vardy?

13 ANSWER

England goalkeeper Jordan Pickford joined Everton from which club?

14 ANSWER

What nationality is Southampton manager Ralph Hasenhuttl?

15 ANSWER

Brighton midfielder Joel Veltman plays international football for which country?

16 ANSWER

Other than Crystal Palace which other Premier League side has Wilfried Zaha played for?

17 ANSWER

At which club was Jurgen Klopp managing before taking over at Anfield?

18 ANSWER

Which kit manufacturer produces Manchester City's 2020/21 playing strip?

19 ANSWER

What nationality is West Ham 'keeper Lukasz Fabianski?

20 ANSWER

V KIDS

Challenge your favourite grown-up and find out which of you is the biggest Premier League brain! The adults' questions are on the left page and the kids' questions are on the right page.

What is the name of Sheffield United's home stadium?

11 ANSWER

How many teams make up the Premier League?

12 ANSWER

Who were the first club to win the Premier League title?

13 ANSWER

Which Premier League club has the nickname 'the Foxes'?

14 ANSWER

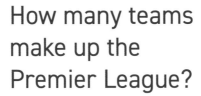

England captain Harry Kane plays his club football for which team?

15 ANSWER

Current Arsenal manager Mikel Arteta is a former Gunners player – true or false?

16 ANSWER

Who is Liverpool's captain?

17 ANSWER

Which London club play their home matches at the London Stadium?

18 ANSWER

How many clubs are relegated from the Premier League each season?

19 ANSWER

What nationality is Manchester City midfielder Kevin De Bruyne?

20 ANSWER

51

ANSWERS ON PAGE 62

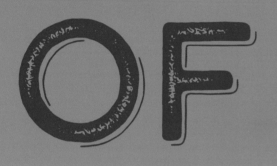

BOYS OF '17

The success of Albion's promotion-winning team of 2016/17 speaks volumes not only for the side's ability but also their mental strength, having fought back from what could have been a knock-out blow the previous season.

A 1-1 draw at Middlesbrough on the final day meant Albion missed out on automatic promotion by just two goals, while injuries and suspensions left the side on the wrong end of a Play-Off semi-final defeat to Sheffield Wednesday.

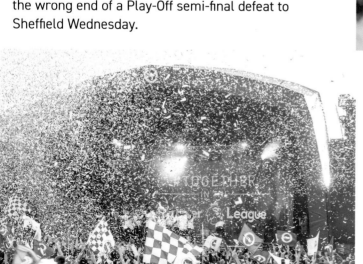

Lesser teams could have crumbled in the face of such disappointment, but Chris Hughton's team came back determined to right the wrongs - and to help them over the line, prodigal son Glenn Murray returned to the club after a five-year absence.

Albion sat mid-table in September, following a 2-0 home defeat against Brentford, but an impressive 18-game unbeaten league run - which included a five-match festive winning streak - saw the side sitting top of the table and two points clear of Newcastle United.

STAR PERFORMER
ANTHONY
KNOCKAERT

Knockaert was named the EFL Championship Player of the Year following a memorable campaign for the Seagulls. A thorn in the side of defences up and down the country, his electric form on the wing was also complemented by 15 league goals - including doubles against Sheffield Wednesday and at Wolves.

A popular figure in the squad, 'Knocky' sadly lost his father that season and the team showed their love when Steve Sidwell scored a memorable goal from the halfway line at Bristol City in November, and the team celebrated the goal by raising Knockaert's shirt as a tribute.

Albion went top with a 2-1 win at Fulham, with 'keeper David Stockdale pulling off a superb penalty save - one of a number of important saves that season. Murray had also scored 15 times by the turn of the year, while fellow strikers Sam Baldock and Tomer Hemed would also reach double figures by the end of the campaign.

Easter proved pivotal, with a four-game winning streak leaving the side on the brink of promotion. It came with a 2-1 home win against Wigan Athletic, where scenes of fans partying on the pitch will live long in the memory. Albion were back in the big time after a 34-year absence.

DAN 33
BURN

POSITION: Defender   **DOB:** 09.05.92
NATIONALITY: English

Arriving from Wigan in August 2018, Dan was immediately loaned back to his former club.

While he returned five months later, he had to wait until the opening game of 2019/20 to make his Premier League debut and excelled in a 3-0 win at Watford. He maintained his form on the left side of defence to become a regular in Graham Potter's side last season.

JOEL 34
VELTMAN

POSITION: Defender   **DOB:** 15.01.92
NATIONALITY: Dutch

Albion's second signing of the summer arrived from Dutch giants Ajax, where he made over 240 appearances.

A versatile defender, he won three Eredivisie titles during his time at the Johan Cruyff Arena and he also appeared in the 2016/17 Europa League final against Manchester United. He made his Netherlands debut against Colombia in November 2013 and has since played over 20 times for his country.

MAX 41
SANDERS

POSITION: Midfielder   **DOB:** 04.01.99
NATIONALITY: English

The central midfielder made his professional bow on loan at AFC Wimbledon, where he was a regular in the side in 2019/20.

He returned to the Amex in the summer of 2020 and went on to make his Albion debut against Portsmouth in the Carabao Cup. He also made his first start in the same competition, at Preston, in the next round.

49 JAYSON
MOLUMBY

POSITION: Midfielder   **DOB:** 06.08.99
NATIONALITY: Irish

The Republic of Ireland international made his Albion debut in a League Cup tie against Barnet in August 2017.

He spent last season on loan at Championship side Millwall and made 40 appearances for the Lions.

Returning to the Albion, his first appearances of the season came against Portsmouth and Manchester United in the Carabao Cup.

JARGON BUSTER

Here is a list of footy jargon. All but one of the terms are hidden in the grid...

...can you work out which is missing?

All To Play For

Back Of The Net

Bags Of Pace

Big Game Player

Box-To-Box

Class Act

Derby Day

Dinked In

Early Doors

Funny Old Game

Game Of Two Halves

Handbags

Hat-Trick

Hollywood Pass

Keep It Tight

Massive Game

Midfield General

Natural Goalscorer

Row Z

Worldy

```
A S M Z U C E M A G E V I S S A M
V A W T B X O W A C V T S V Y B N
P O I B Y D I N K E D I N B R Q A
R L Q C J K X Z E F M L F J N E T
O G F W K C I R T T A H C S A Z U
E X B H D A V A P N H X G B J E R
T K A L L T O P L A Y F O R D C A
I R C P M E Q M O L R X G H O A L
F L K D N U R A S T T P K Q C P G
U F O N Z Y D I W O M W Y I B F O
N H F W Z O E S B B U N E H L O A
N J T G O B N O D F F X K A D S L
Y Z H S V R X M A G V O R N I G S
O X E A D C L H H G A E U D Z A C
L B N K Q J L D C J N K A B I B O
D D E R B Y D A Y E E S P A L B R
G W T E U O I P G J I O J G S M E
A C I O K I R D Y U X K T S F A R
M H W V Y B L T B P C H F O R R A
E O P C D E E T G E G Q B L P E N
V G C M I H A F M I E K Y V Z G L
H J B F D W A R T X I D H D C T D
L X D M O A S T A S O L G A T A R
V I A Q K Y I H S O D W J H Y A Q
M P F E Z P R G R G U N F M I S G
Z I N Q E J N S L J P I K Z Y S O
D B S E V L A H O W T F O E M A G
E K T X S L T E M X K W U L L C I
U S N Q L U W E A B V R S P C O B
A Y O R S F I T W Y O T A N B M I
H O L L Y W O O D P A S S U T I
```

56

ANSWERS ON PAGE 62

AARON
CONNOLLY

BRIGHTON & HOVE ALBION

Want to leap like Mat Ryan, have the strength of Lewis Dunk or boast the endurance of Tariq Lamptey? Build up your strength for action with our...

30 DAY

Day 1
Right let's get started! 10 squats, 25 star jumps, 10 sit-ups - all before school!

Day 2
Make your mum a brew before going out to practice your keepy-uppys

Day 3
10 squats
50 star jumps
10 sit-ups

Day 4
How about swapping the crisps in your lunchbox for an apple?

Day 5
Take a one mile ride on your bike

Day 6
75 star jumps
15 sit-ups
15 press-ups

Day 7
Help clean the car before going out to play headers and volleys with your friends

Day 8
75 star jumps
15 sit-ups
15 press-ups
Before and after school now!

Day 9
Walk to school rather than take the bus

Day 10
Head to the swimming pool for a 30-minute swim

Day 11
100 star jumps
20 sit-ups
20 press-ups
Twice a day now, don't forget!

Day 12
Make sure you trade one of your fizzy drinks for a glass of water today

Day 13
Jog to the shop for your mum... before playing any video games!

Day 14
Give a hand around the house before kicking your ball against the wall 500 times

Day 15
Time to increase those exercises!
25 squats
25 sit-ups
25 press-ups
Before and after school!

Day 16
Take a nice paced two-mile jog today

Day 17
25 squats
150 star jumps
25 press-ups
Remember, before and after school

Day 18
Cycle to school rather than rely on the bus or a lift

Day 19
30 squats
150 star jumps
30 press-ups
Twice a day too!

Day 20
Get out and practice those free-kicks, practice makes perfect remember...

Day 21
Get peddling! Time for a two-mile trip on two wheels today

Day 22
Upping the workload now...
40 squats, 40 sit-ups
40 press-ups
Before and after school!

Day 23
Wave goodbye to the chips - ask for a nice salad for lunch today

Day 24
40 squats
40 sit-ups
40 press-ups
Twice a day, don't forget...

Day 25
Time to get pounding the streets - the jogging is up to three miles today

Day 26
45 star jumps
45 sit-ups
45 press-ups

Day 27
Time to swap those sweets and biscuits for some fruit

Day 28
45 star jumps
45 sit-ups
45 press-ups

Day 29
You're getting fitter and fitter now! Keep up the squats and star jumps plus join an after-school sports club - ideally football!

Day 30
Well done - you made it!
50 squats, 50 sit-ups and 50 press-ups!
These are the core ingredients to your success

CHALLENGE
to improve your all-round footy fitness!

WHAT BALL?

Can you figure out what ball is the real one in each photo?

ANSWERS ON PAGE 62

SOLLY
MARCH

ANSWERS

PAGE 16 · ADULTS V KIDS

Adults

1. Conor Coady. 2. Arsenal, Chelsea, Manchester City and Manchester United. 3. Derby County. 4. Roy Hodgson, Crystal Palace. 5. AFC Bournemouth. 6. Sporting Lisbon. 7. Gillingham. 8. Four – Blackburn Rovers, Liverpool, Manchester City and Manchester United. 9. Arsenal. 10. Frank Lampard, Chelsea.

Kids

1. Liverpool. 2. German. 3. Five – Leeds United, Manchester United, Newcastle United, Sheffield United and West Ham United. 4. Wolverhampton Wanderers. 5. Manchester United/Old Trafford. 6. Manchester City. 7. The Toffees. 8. Newcastle United. 9. Brendan Rodgers. 10. Portuguese.

PAGE 20 · WHO ARE YA?

1. Alexis Mac Allister. 2. Aaron Connolly.
3. Ben White. 4. Solly March.
5. Lewis Dunk. 6. Adam Lallana.
7. Pascal Gross. 8. Dan Burn.
9. Yves Bissouma. 10. Adam Webster.
11. Tariq Lamptey.

PAGE 40
CLASSIC FANTASTIC →

PAGE 43
SPOT THE DIFFERENCE →

PAGE 50 · ADULTS V KIDS

Adults

11. Chelsea. 12. Sean Dyche, Burnley.
13. Fleetwood Town. 14. Sunderland. 15. Austrian.
16. The Netherlands. 17. Manchester United.
18. Borussia Dortmund. 19. Puma. 20. Polish.

Kids

11. Bramall Lane. 12. 20 teams. 13. Manchester United. 14. Leicester City. 15. Tottenham Hotspur.
16. True. 17. Jordan Henderson. 18. West Ham United.
19. Three. 20. Belgian.

PAGE 56 · JARGON BUSTER

Big Game Player

PAGE 60 · WHAT BALL?

TOP: Ball G.
BOTTOM: Ball F.

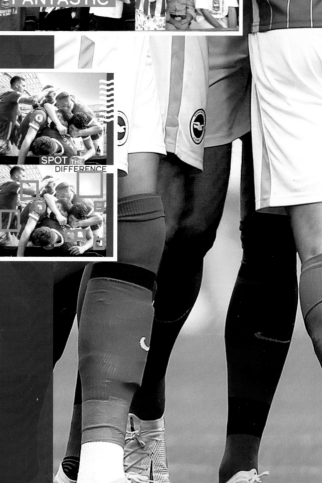